KUIR ë GARANG

The Carcass Valley

TNP

The Nile Press
Calgary, Alberta

First TNP Edition 2015

ISBN: 978-0-9938279-4-5

PUBLISHED BY THE NILE PRESS
http://www.thenilepress.com
Calgary
Printed in USA

PREFACE

Without ideas, experiences and our reflection on them, life would be irksomely boring. Ideas sometimes make life a revolving ball of plight, and sometimes an island of unexplored riches. People have ideas. Some people don't know what to do with them but others appreciate them to the required height. Those who lend the required glances at their ideas use them for the betterment of what they live for. However, others trash the desired elements of their cognitive endowment for they see nothing beneficial in their thoughts. "But strange as it may appear," Edmund Burke (1765: 323) wrote, "we are always at a loss to know what ideas we have of things, or whether we have any ideas at all upon some objects."

Be it bad or good, life always gives people something to reflect on however boring it [life] is or has been. This 'something' could be objects or experiences that constitute or furnish our ideas pool; ideas we use to tackle the word. Without such object-engendered experiences and their resultant ideas, our epistemic reality would be really vacuous (Ayers, 2001; Locke, 1836).

Those who live a relatively calm and privileged life tend to ignore the fact that every minute lived is worth *the* pen. It is indeed unfortunate that human experiential reflections, most of the time, dwells on experiences with bitterness than sweetness. Nonetheless, bitterness and shocking experiences—taken in a very clean and constructive heartiness—can change or enrich one's life's direction.

The collection of the poems in *Carcass Valley* covers a wide range of topics. These include plight as a result of war, sweetness and bitterness of love, despair and defiance in life, hope, loss, and other elements of cosmic repulsiveness.

Given my personal experiences since I was just three, this collection is informed by what it is like to be a child on the move, a child who searches for meaning in life when no one helps him get answers, a child who gropes for something when that *something* escapes him yet he still tries day and night to frisk for it.

The question of personal loss and tragedies, my reflection on life experiences about South Sudan and Africa and their connection to the rest of the world, feature prominently in the collection. Those who don't enjoy poetry will still leave with a line (if not a verse) that will imprint an indelible mark of thoughts bewilderment.

I am presenting a word to those who govern and those who are governed; those who are subjugated and those who subjugate; those who hate and whose are objects of hate, the center and the periphery

Lastly, I mourn the loss of my father and celebrate his life for he taught me to see the struggle in life as lessons for possible productivity. This loss and celebration leads to my philosophical reflection on my experiences and abstract ideas.

Kuir ë Garang
Calgary, Alberta
March 7, 2015

Citations

Burke, E. (1756). *A Philosophical Enquiry Into the Origin of Our Ideas of the Sublime and the Beautiful,* London: J. Dosley.

Ayers, M. (2001). *Locke: Epistemology and Ontology*, New York: Routledge.

Locke, J. (1836*). An Essay Concerning Human Understand ing:* London: T. Tegg and Sons.

This is dedicated to my late father, *Garang Kuir Ajak* from whom I learned to see life's struggle as a blessing.

PART I

LOVE AND LIFE

Sunflower

She saw that sunflower when
The gardener glided the mower over it.
It was the day after her birthday.

The day I left her by the roadside
And summer's palms weren't in debacle.
They were laying fun in a scrumptious flow.

Though she hadn't picked it up
For interference, she had framed
Its charms and elegance just
By her primary rubberneck.

When I saw her a year later, nestled
Desirously just inside the crook
Of my arms, she poured the story to me
 With wits, vivacity, clarity
And enviable brevity.

Like a product of a pious womb
And queens of the ancient darks souls,
She shot up and presented a boxed mystery:
"Me, I and my own!"

I thought a gift it was, but gee!
It was a year-old sunflower.

Serenade #1

City night

We'll sip the
Nectarine juice
And inhale mirth,
Rosy aromas...
As if we've been for ages.

We'll squat, amazed
At the city's riches,
That pump up the need
To have our fingers
Dovetailed...

We'll get up the loftier
Of the town scrapers and rule
The night, telling the
Moon to maintain
Her quirky and curvy grin.

Romance wings

We'll steal away from
The city's hate, to the warmth
Of the sky, stars blinking,
Winking, giggling as they
Marvel, envious of
This closeness, our closeness.

Love guides

We'll fly away, telling
Seraph to guide us
To where love rules,

16

Daring not a come back
To this changeable
Cosmic conundrum:
Ironical!

She'll lead us to the
Highest of all mountains,
Where air is fresh, oxygen
Thin but clear, trees never dry,
Grass never change colour
Roses not watered.
There, we, they, will smile with
Satisfaction!

Spices of our sojourn

Our sojourn sermonized
By your crispy cute-ness
And wonders of this
Freshness, we'll soar
Over airs, float over
The darkest, brightest of
Clouds,

And float over
Seas and oceans, the
Earth's will trillion
Times far, deep in hate
And confusion'...
Will we take it?
It's love!

The Artic Night and You

I sat on the couch in the balcony
Just but thinking. Was eight o' clock!
My pen had refused to ink down
To grace on this paper, to bestow to
The beauty of upper craving. All the
Grassy eyes as my nocturnal imagination.

As I stared at the blankness of the sky,
Riveted by your present ghosts, your
Apocryphal presence erased the stars,
And the glamour of the then sprinkles of stars,
That were as bright as the desire
In me to blink at you once again.

It was not a game yet a game, but...
Although the night looked the same,
Thoughts of you created a cloud of
Non-existence like nothingness, like
I just didn't exist: just to speak of mirage.

As the moon blinked at my craving
Desire and embraces the Artic horizon,
Spreading its ridiculous yet niggling
Consoling light, I saw you, sitting on
The couch, not like me,

You breathed in the help of the sun,
Watched the swarm of kites as children
Warmed and swarm the shore, I hoped I would
See them again, but the thought of you
Kept me on a battered life's boat,
My heart and thought of you
Reminded me of disturbing thoughts,

But as the day broke, I felt Deng's hand
On my shoulder! It is morning did you
Sleep her (e), he said. Like a wounded lioness,
Like a drunk drinking you all night, I got up,
But I knew it wasn't to be that short.

The Charm of the Oriental

With body as soft and tender as a baby's touch,
And heart so small yet so kind,
Welcoming, the messianic speech time,
I wonder whose heart her lips touch,
Drinking all that smoothness from the angel.

With hip defying meticulous nature sculpture,
And natures quarrelling as to who curved
The frame, planting the breasts for the served
Who giggle when guarded - embraced by culture,
 Vividly preserved on the true angel.

Her bosom flowery as spring roses,
Comforting you as if mummy embraced.
She holds you tight - protected and graced
As you drift into deep sleep with goodness doses,
 From your true angel.

Her shyness campaigns rare novelty
In the peak of calculated and stolen glances,
And a frame so tempting – attraction balances.
With her enviable touch your itchy hand plans
To run your trembling fingers over the true angel.

Serenade # 2

Take only one of my hands and squeeze it,
Touch my elbow; bend it from the crook,
Pull me to you but don't move an inch,
Look into my eyes and don't wink away the grace,
Smile to me and don't bend your head to the sides,
Speak to me but don't change your sweetest chirp,
Laugh with me but don't leave me laughing,
Touch my lips but don't kiss me dead,
Lead me home as if it's for you,
Sing with me but don't sing my name,
Walk next to me, your being ahead sedates me,
Lean on me if your love strengthens me,
Hold me tight, assemble me,
I'm pieces without you.

The Voice

I saw you that day of that nameless wedding,
Standing under a meaningless tree by the church
Window, the church's green-yellow pane losing your dress,
Then I heard your voice before the bell gong.
 It wasn't to wane nor lost; it became me.

Me! As that voice, absorptive, clear in my mind
And heart, now though far, far away
In the grappler, in that meridian hand, in the guidance
Of hunch that you give and be given,

                    You called.

Earnestly, like a thirsty *thiang* in African dry time,
I sip in every atom of goodness you say,
Gluing me to my couch as my soul dance
To the tune of your charms, that with time deepens.

Though your voice is humbly low you say 'you're mine!'
To fill the emptiness in my room with 'it's okay!'
Words so simple yet so potent; putting me on balance
As that melodious, soulful voice, slings you deep in.

Good Things

A pigeon perched
On my rusted iron
Balcony.
I told him
To ease his look…
'Screw you!' he looked
Like saying,
Infuriated by
This solid insolence, I raised
My arm to act, but he
Turned me that puffy and rude tail…
When I checked the neighbour's
Balcony, adorned with crimson,
Bloodless, and violet
Strings of floweret vases…there! stood
A charm, well… holding some floral teeth…
Oh yeah, I wanted the pigeon there…
But hey! He'd already fled.

Coquette? No!

You will sit by me with that fancy negligee.
You'll sip your juice with a desire key
As you chortle when I footle and can't see,
That jewel, that you're a chorister of valentine:

You hold a dove and a light vivacious candela,
Wearing a purple skirt and a solace umbrella,
Your tongue atop a wine glass and life novella
In hand, you defy life, the groove of Stella.

PART II

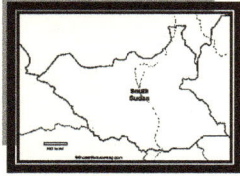

POEMS ABOUT SOUTH SUDAN

The Carcass Valley

I walked *The Carcass Valley* where
Damning heat's fury is never pacified.
Unresolved past then thought was the pride,
Had selfishness agree with the valley's clime,
Making *The Carcass Valley* the father of all rages,
Where simple happiness costs more than
Sweetness of life else where.

I have been told the stories of *The Carcass Valley*,
Sitting by my father's side, his metal, rubber
And canvass chair, placing him above all...
All eating his story with pride and passion,
It was a line of serenity, abundance, joy and tribal
Pride: greenness stretched the furthest the eye saw,
Elegant vista, dotted sparingly with required
Beautifying elements of the valley's trees,

Then came human *will,* balloons inflated with
Air of contempt and jealousy, from lands where
Abundance was not a *word* in comfort lexicon,
These simpletons came from far away lands...
In a jealous blink the greenness vanished
Just like a good dream melting away come morning,
And like the morning dews evaporating on smelling
The sunrays...the valley's meaning was gone,

As if the valley wasn't addled enough, burned and
Cleared of ancestral significance: content ripped
And annihilated in a 'bad faith' purposed pretense.
Then the bad world of the man's hands coughed...
Oppressed voices of valley and the savannah
Sounded their trumpets: the little remains

Of the good valley be spared, they'd thought.
 But the *man's hand* mowed them and spread them on
 the valley: from away, from the land, the jealous, the happy,
The protective:
They filled the valley with bones and charcoal
of human bones, burnt in delight, rage and suicide,

Then rose their souls, coiling upward like smoke
In a still windless afternoon, the searing sunrays followed
By the tropical rain, the valley breed tragedy of harmed
Spirit of the land, diseases, genocide and racial harm,
The greenish beauty of *The Carcass Valley*...
Became the carcass of the voices and the altruistic.

After *The* Peace

In a wearying wind she wonders around the crane,
Musing to heaven, stars, and her feel into thoughts drain.

Short, slim, dark and small, she smiles looking over the lea,
Like a sedated patient, she stood, her arms spread facing the lee.

Never worries, lives back, serenity claimed, she wants to eat nature,
Nature that is only but a feel, it's beauty she missed, her soul pasture.

She had a crumpled soul, now a cleansed pride, an emptied heart
Ready to fill with new love, then, coerced and accepted, it was a hard,

Fear of mockery exonerated, she let go their deeds, and lick raindrops
On her and the savannah leaves, with the new quiet she needs good stops.

Biting Haricot

She'll elegantly ride a *gold horse* in the plain
Of her ancestral ghosts, joyously biting haricot
As her ride sways smoothly, historical claims
That for ages she wanted to see, not
Strutting, yet doing so in her inner chambers, sprain
Of her then mocked conscience evaporated, not a spot--
Clean like spirit in a blowing in wind, not a chain--
One that has always covered her shines, strong *will* got
Shining even when stifled... but now shines openly, the main
Embodiment of hell set on fire to burn, hot
But not in the real sense of mundane
Nonsense...it was the *will* preserved that got her jot
And engrave ill-fated, murky, sordid ideas of her same
Image, then caricatured, but now she sips honey and blows mot
For bees that reared the bees, she cuts *manga* at no lame
Cost, fishes with no restraint, eats with no bills but not
For her assumed lazy hand...she's now freed.

The Sudd

This black *sheet* was sewn
Even if I can't see the seams,
It might have been a work
Of a skilled seamstress,
Now it is always desired.
The care-takers of the sheet
Only watch it and stand aside
To see the 'owners' use it...
Swampy, dumb, dark and 'rich,'
Even if there's nothing in it,
I'll still fish there if not warned,
Enjoying the rhino's laughs and
Crocodiles coughing a welcome.

I will be that man, the needy one,
The fisher who pegs his hopes on it,
Then turns and says, "even if the heaviest
Of the heaviest meteorites
Envies this enviable corner
And visits with a thunderous scare,
It'll not drain it dry on my helpless watch,
I'll flatten my energies and resolves: me first!
Then drain it dry, giving me more...
Or making me *done-done* to float!"

The Real Sons

They were behind the lorry hanging like monkeys,
On the unlucky tree on which they were bundled up.
Then a fat, short man stole the car keys
Saying he hadn't eaten. But a big streak
Of smoked meat was stuck to his teeth, a stick
In hand where he had the meat, voices in front
Said he was stoned, but he should beatify the fond...

The driver, a lady with a heart believed that mouth
Whose uncle ruled the hind county: the *south*
Citizens' agony, exploits, laughs all to his round belly.
How I wished a slight cramp for his bag, he wolfed-in daily,
The lopsided affairs of the land and the country weren't his,
But they'd *drained* the nation in the way they pleased.

For the fat man and his uncle death was fun
They crossed their fingers and the fight went on,
I'd rather have them to the bin but they're not done,
Any deed against them fainted with their nonentity, only fried
Feat is their essence, like starved lions they always cried
To widen their open jaws...really wide!
But then I came home a year later
On the same hilly greenness, the foggy skies, the crater...
The same *wolf* spread his fat bottom, rumbling in a revolving chair:
'What you want sa?'

After Bellicose Hearts

It is only a land but I will sleep on it,
It is only grass but I will keep it green,
It is only a river but I will swim in it,
It is only a swamp but I will keep it,
It is only trees but I will sit under them,
The mosquitoes bless me the more...
It is only treks but I will make bare-footed paths,
Mum I'll leave not because of *the* land...

Instead of guns I want a pen,
And for the barrack I need prayer-line,
And for the tanks I will buy lorries,
For the prayer I will choose not to destroy,
For the landmines I will have yams,
And for the gods I will not scream, scream, scream!
For I know the gods are not weak,
Clearly I am not the gods' guardian.
And for the country the artic mercies will sashay me,
And all will sacrifice over the land
But I will leave not mum, because of the land.

I cry but the tears are less than the cause to cry for,
I have so much laugh but all is hammered in me,
The crescent and the star will never understand,
The cross sings of helpful brotherhood,
That cross saddens me but I squeeze out laughter,
Tall definitions aimed but existential depths I dig,
Structured, preserved and honoured...
So I'll leave not mum because of the land.

I Will Bury It On My Barren Canal

When the sound of terror melts away,
And the then smoked and mocked leftovers
Of twenty years of paralysis come out
Of their hidings, I will stand on the canal
And gaze over its stretching barrenness, barrenness that
Breeds nothing but utter emptiness and hopelessness.
That, I will now stretch into abundance of my
Mouth's fill to let go the fangs of misery and mockery:
Mockery—natural and man-made—that placed
Me against my heart's and nature's directives,
Because I bred and breed no known semblance,
Thought no enduring fruition: social and intellectual,
Yet I'm important for nothing well defined,
 Still indispensable like goodness of servant to
The master, excellently good yet slow.
But as I stand on the canal, gazing defiantly
Over the Eastern horizon, where the red-yellow
Africa sun rolls into the clear blue sky, sky so bright
And clear, so beautiful yet content so scotching like
The land I'm standing on,
So clear and fertile yet offering me nothing to swallow.
Then I look over my shoulder, still on the same
Canal, I swing my gun, that they say I need not now,
The *cause* of everything that burnt me, left me emptiness, left
my
Soil crying for plants, left me alone, with nothing to clink to:
No siblings, no mum, no dad: all swallowed by the soil,
The soil that needed something to hold, to feed on
Because it was not planted on,
I was knifed by hunger because the soil was abandoned,
It was emptied, burnt by my gun; a gun that was given me.
They said it'd protect me but then it finished me.

34

Cartridges No More

The crystalline quartz glass
Will be cracked at last.
The shade, mood, stir
Will be calmed by the epical *heir*.
As gloaters count misfortune
To rip the then chicanery opportune
And head the new chivalric grits,
They'll 'honour' the deceived then breaks to fits
And starts, hoisting hullabaloo
To the loftiest note around igloo
Looking mud-hut, ringing
Circling, sighing, singing
By joy, cry, wishing it never goes
Now that the metal killer echoes
Cryptic repudiation, it now seeks
To squeeze through. These slicks
Feign to forge cohesiveness,
Then comes discerned sleekness.
Deceptive! Slicker, not indecisive,
Perhaps, motherly deceptive,
Draining still, slicker still, not indecisive
But soaked in caprice,
Because the first morning rays will kiss the price
And holds proudly conspicuous the flag
To the Eastern, Southern Sun. Not to snag,
As the weakling run with chickenhearted-ness,
The holders will mourn its seen truthfulness,
But when the bull picks the run
The fighter picks the gun,
No guns go gust, but
Where will the doubt be?

The Deprived and the Helpers

The dawn of the morning
Is followed by nothing but mourning,
But why is there no one to blame
When all is on the other side and not the same?
Maybe it is what they are meant to have,
Nearing or in fact claimed by the cave.

The dawn of the morning
Again comes with all the frowning,
But they hope that altruism still exists,
For some—like angels—provide when all else desists,
God! Is that who they really are—providers or sympathizers?
They're left to crave for trivialities when the world talks dia-
pers!

The dawn of the morning
Impregnated by ideas comes scorning,
But who it plays tricks with when dichotomy
Of their being hides the truth? does it show the e'nomy?
That's the food for my mind and yours too.
The explorers sing the deprived plight
But get the ghastly scene when the screen...

The Singer

"Everything deteriorated stealthily
But it will beam back happily,"
He had sung, his spears glittering,
His lavender loincloth tired and aging.

He'd knifed the air above the moo
Of the camp, lordly voice with no
Cheap pride…neither an epitome of ailing
Ancient kings' lisping, who were killing
By choice, for pleasure (fear) and dislike,

He'd seen the fabric, the web of greed scattered
By some arsonists. Right! Leaders faltered.
The big men feigned strength and the destiny
Building. Sure they will go home, the prodigy
had seen *peace*.

Is Freedom Not Sweet?

Fake it not 'cause I'm coming,
Like hurricane you'll see me charming,
Hate me now for there will be no time
For you to practice my down for dime.

You will carry me shoulder high,
As if I've never heard you before sigh.
With all the niceties now gone you wonder
If it's time for you be kept there fixed under.

Vengeance is not a good virtue,
But tell me the meaning of this statue
That all carry *me* meaning *you!*
You will tell the world now freedom
Has served the owner, and you should
Watch the Nile ruled by the sons and daughters.

Before Harvests

Ever-green and untouched,
The twilight congregation
Of their leaves moonlight reflection
Defies the night's darkness blanket.
So healthy,
So promising,
The farmer grins
As he plants a scarecrow next to
The coconut tree, between
the footpath ploughed
On its both flanks...
The moon sails jubilantly above
And he smiles with preponderance
Of satisfaction, a month
to come, he will sing with the
birds, the early ones, and hopes
That no Owl invades.

PART III

SUFFERING AND ENDURANCE

After the Delos Mission

They have been firm in voices and steps.
They have graced and placed the strait
Under those hard smiles: hidden but jazzy.

The straight flow of *slight hydra*, the peeves
Of premonition bore eternity and were straight,
But the wait was crippling as a cliff edge, and hazy.

They wore paints of defiance, but the reps
Of narratives exhorted them, exemplified by brait,
They were gazing; waiting for the end, it was still fuzzy

They begged for mercies to end them, mercies
Waned, mercies surged, mercies vanished
Like spirit in the wind, and time famished,

Time famished and sickened, social heresies
Counted for none, the grace in war stood unblemished
When the dry wind of the end blew; jocosely finished.

Amateurs entertained the drums, jalousies
Of end and continuity stood face to face, relished
Synthetic braveries swarmed before the end clinched,

So well clinched that the end dread was *praises*.
Even if they knew it no longer, onlookers relinquished
Not their stamp, now dogmatised defiance so wished!

Surmise

The inculcated wish made the belief,
Perhaps the marble envy to sing
That all stones there are, are fixed
And all can move them not.

But humane chores are not
Suggested, they should inhere in
Beliefs: external and intrinsic
Like seasonal acceptances,
Their advance not doubted...

Beliefs? But all have been reticent,
Never laying the fame but
The survival feats in the churches!
It's stream of conformity,
Everlasting after the priest,

When it's spring winter is sung,
Summer, spring it is, diamond
Is the worthless of pearls, donkey
Barks and dogs bray.

Surely, even if there is a *gold breather*,
It will serve none supposed.
Ask all their own selves,
Structural and genteel,
Fresh air and wishes.
Natures will clamour and extend
A long blessed hand, to say a want,
A want like that; and for it they will pray, and eat.
As all streams to the chief-stream.

Karma

Forget the nervous veins; bunk worries'
Tremors. Obscurity of volition will be
The steel of lion's claim to grits bestowal,
Bestowal engraved *on* as providence's karma.
It would be said!

Pay and wish to decolour the bestowal
When it becomes the crystalline epic,
Historical king, defining the sun's direction,
The temple front and churchmen *wills* and bells gong.

That will spray blessings on the closed paths, the ways of
Red-hot, yellowish, amber, fright-inducing steel, the avoidance
Of gloom when the dark bishop prays.

In the shade there's a scotching shower of the sun's anger,
In architectural soundness there's a feeling of being
drenched in a month-long torturous torrent,
This is a less dreaded conscience's
Marriage to timeless queries.

The Girdle

Wallace stood reflective yet enduring
In that isolated storeys of old tales' reverberations,
The only place they number a handful...
Big and ruling, balling, 'happily' feeling...
But he grasped less all which *dad* in his last breathing
Said to him, that he had home, the world:

"You ain't belong here son, you own the world,
by line, by word, by dope, by valour..."

Rules' wounds couldn't let him finish the wish.
Now Wallace tries to connect the dots, with zest
And iron strength he knew he owns the world,
A lion ruling the jungle but what world?
His dad's word guided him through the broken life,
But that ruling the world landed him in *that* box,
Hated for strength and trials:
Friend and foes alike!
Honour and dread whisper alike,
But Wallace...
Knew he was true *tropics* yet a true *Columbian*,
Columbian by birth and axiom, Southerner by blood
And choice, yet none seem welcoming.
Maybe he just imagined; but why think in
That box? Maybe it reminded him of the ancestral
Middle passage, maybe that is why they
Still get fished and boxed, still seared!
Revered, severed and placed there to beards!
Though still as innocent as sky knows,
And as strong as the first *uncle* landed.
He wondered if he'd begrudged the sky:
Eastwards, westwards, southwards, northwards,
And a cinnamon soul laughs go just
But to the refined heights,
The conspicuous and crystal nightmares

46

Called for a roommate, and by gods,
He stays by the corner to be *The One.*

Chicanery

Near that yellowish dotted
Door of his silver
Rimed and louvered window,
Stood a ragged ten-year-old,
Like a sixth century leftover
Of dehumanizing plagues,
With image showing
Of a body-like figure,
Bent like a showy and
Skilled contortionist,
Pounded by pestles
Of hunger...
But *he* indifferently opened his
Radio and called his cook:
Not a word, he told the cook,
Bewildered and dazed,
The cook marvelled and eyed
Pityingly the kid, who upon
Time there with no response, no
Nothing, carried her
Wire-like thinness away, daring
Not to look back, struggling
With the wind, the dust, and the
Inside punches of hunger.
There again stood *he,* by
The window watching her
Blowing away and said:
I am not everybody's keeper,
With those words she collapsed,
Taken with grace...emaciated...
Then there came *he,* running, crying:
She left before I saw her, he said,
God why? Cried he,

But like a crocodile, who'll ever know?
Everyone believed him, a 'good' man,
The cook was quiet: 'cause poverty
Told him to keep his job.

Ain't Nobody

I wasn't born there, but . . .
But you see *me*, ain't nothing
You can say. . .I am the *Nile, Kemet*. . .
Put Eric, my last name, and there I vanish,
Put John, my first name, and there 'I shine.'

I am not in want of going home,
So you think I don't belong there:
'Why praise *it* but still glued here?'
You have asked that over and again.

I might not know how to
Polish that spear sparklingly clean,
Not initiated with my *Kemetic* peers,
But I see my face when I put her before me,
It's not just what I say. . .*monstrous proofs!*
Like that mirror in your room,
It's crystal and spotless resemblance,
It subsumes no wishful thinking
It's sublimity over your corpus disses,

I might be a little at odd with that trueness,
But you see that organic beauty,
Her humility. . .
She sits in wait for all of us, even *you*,
She gives all her room and soaks in the rain,
Gives all her land and works for her visitors;
Even me. . .
I am here, far away, comfortable,
But her plight I cut a piece of.

I hear you say I am her daughter,

It's what you hear her say,
Indeed, I was consciously spoilt,
I don't have her true perfection,
You and I spoilt her...
I spoilt myself for worse,
I'd hated her image, you'd said,
Time and again...you'd said!
But you'd chided and cheated me.
Now the veil is off...I see!

I still seem to hate her but I've known...
Now the veil is off...I see!
I'll always *be* her though different inside out,
I'll cherish her grits and put her before me
And see my face...
Ain't nobody...yes, ain't nobody
Gonna hoodwink me no more.
I'll always sing this song!

Jonglei Kids

At a clear distance
Of Nilotic plain dry season,
At the mercy of the mirage,
I sighted cattle camp kids,
As white as pallid artic kids
Under varied coloration
Of the dance club lights,
And a Native American
Under the neon street light
Holding his cup to any
Secular Samaritan.
There the kids scuttled, wizened
By the heat and the cold, wearing
Nothing but gods' mercies,
But I didn't know why they looked white?
As 'black' as miners' clothes in Azania's
Coalmine fields they naturally were,
I couldn't guess the least!
Then came them near, suffused
By the *arou*, their skins hardened
By prolonged exposure to nature's bites.
Even as teenagers, they were middle-aged men.

Under a Mango Tree

Make me go with you please,
And I will not be the same me,
Because all that I dreamt of and
Pin my hope on, was to see my hand
Mirrored, and helpful.

When I come back full and increased,
And sit on the Nile bank, under a tree,
A mango tree, throwing mud at the
Dancing crocodiles and sipping in
The breeze of the Nile collection,
Which I see and feel: the greenish
Beauty of the Nilotic sooty sudd...
I'll be the jolly fellow.

Then the mooing cattle will wear away
My worries as the young naked kids
Play with the dried and burnt cow dung,
Beautifying their bare bodies with varied colours
To look like jubilant red ants on
An after-rain African evening.

I will stop there, because, like
A lioness charging after spoiling
Wardens, I will sit on a mat in
A furiously pouring rain that's
Hailing cups and sacks of ice,
And tell it that it's its chance to take
The last kick, because I have been
Filled and increased, and I will
No long be beaten, but I will
Always sit under *my* mango tree.

Gone with the Nile

She sat on the riverbank,
Her waist as slender as
Wasp's own, and looked
At her face, dark like unrefined
Microcrystalline African diamond,
So beautiful and innocent like she was
Moulded from the darkest
African soil by the skilled
And humblest
Of all artists.

With her breasts bare, erect,
Rich and naively nature's natural,

She wound the rag on
Her lower self and played
With the ripples formed
By the gentle rain drops
And the friendly baby fish,
She sat still, feeling the rumble
Of the thunder in a distance,
Rumbling like a dying sound
of receding enemy arsenal.

But as she fetched her take,
She was fetched, and there
She was gone with the Nile.

Fizzled Efforts

To see all gone
Till he used the
Bayonet.

To set his course,
Wanting to enjoy
His making, but
Out it all fizzled.

Having no soul,
A heart, a figure—
He cribbed the
Neighbour's efforts:

The daft effort
Now flying as his
Pylon; a cretonne
That defies distances.

As The World Passes Him By

As the world flies by, he [victim] stands still with less, not an iota
Of mechanistic smiles to sigh, a just pause from demeanour
Of megacosm's neoplasm. We will take that for him.

He has less as explicit offer except professing statistics,
A bummer of eternity, enticing the cosmos with it
As a precaution indicator to serve limitlessly the earthliness.

As the world passes him by, and comes back to him
Just to say bye, he joyously breathes in his father's grace...
But the enemy found him, dug a draining canal and sat atop
The crane, only to tell him he can now exist even if the enemy
Washes his fingers to wait for his [victim's] innocent response.

So, we'll ask him how and why; what that twinkle in eagles'
Eyes above is? Why *Nilean* crocodiles scream steady?
Why elephants hop briskly over-looking Kilimanjaro?
Why cranes protest their being in Nakuru as they
Shore him piteous waters? Why the hippos' ride gave him
The cry for laughs?

That's all we'd want him to scream.

So we'll help him defrost the frozen tropical parks,
But Africa is the tropic and no one cauterized her plains,
Not then, not now, not ever...perhaps this is just *bad faith*,
The world eyes her enviously in a deniable pretension,
The nature has perhaps withdrawn from the hued one,
Maybe that's why he stands by, but who could we be?

As the world passes him by he thinks of a graceful offer—
He was then the biblical *alpha* and *omega*: is the world *his* fault?
Now, the then *Upperland* brother is the *Hindland* brother,

56

He consumes our epistemic and politicking with noble silence,
Our constructed and purposed narrative wasn't on his side,
He's given us so much yet he's only some exotica, a ritual…
Nothing competitiveness to give as the world passes him by.

Josephine Never Came Back!

Josephine is sick,
But she can't go home,
Because the work
She has to finish,
Asks her down,
Her superior,
The same:
'Work has to be done
Money has to be made
Not spend anyhow.'
But Josephine is strong…
She finishes *her* work.
But who pays the bill
To the doctor,
The casket,
'The festivities'
The boss?
The parent(s)?
Happiness or sadness?

Turkana Plain

Ragged, wizened and fatigued,
Ekale stared pityingly at
The heads he was guarding,
But like him, they had little
Pasture for food.

With the arid sun knifing
Him mercilessly, he angled
His left leg onto his right thigh and
Then cuffed his right hand over his
Eyebrow to see his heads through
The blinding mirage and scotching haze.

He then let go the leg-fold and lazed
Towards the acacia shade which barely
Offered him any protective shadow.

Even with his rubber-like feet, Ekale still
Suffered burns of the searing and boiling sand,
Bathing in the hellish dust whirled around
In the stormy chaos of desert dryness and anger,
But above all this, Ekale defies nature:
A proud poor soul.

Overstrung

'Stop!' There was a voice out of the dark.
It was mysterious and seriously dark,
Making out that silhouette scared the crow.

And the voice, the voice engendered
Fear and stirred up memories of yester-years' tumult,
When the crows would run helter-skelter.

Growing rambunctious with every control device,
The crow breathed, even the artifices the enemy em-
ployed
Had the crow lift the yolk, the fatigue of our run,
scare.

There wasn't any remedy, but fear became strength,
Night like day, all the same, sun like moon,
The shine was never heeded: it was the match,
The walk, the thirst, and the dirty water
The crow stole and purified,
The half-cooked meat stirred endless
Cramps.

There the crows flew and flew, run and run,
Dodged bullets and mingled with threats:
They had to eat the same jungle the scare manned...
The choice wasn't there, they just got to live:
There was the voice!

At Nethermost

The few line manning my face if you
Ask, aren't beauty creases, if not age
Arrangement and a jubilant gnome airs,
It would be life's toll on me.

Speak of bygone days, and days aren't
Layabouts, they sip one's strength and sail along
At each chance they lick at life's sweetness.
The gaze rather be a glance at days speed!

If dad's lines whined to come and I knew,
I would have been in 'eureka!' to scream praise
To my own self, a 'foiler' of age tunnel:
Smuggling age spoilt, done!
I would be over to watch, where old age
Steals in.
My lines aren't age.
I'm just stressed!

The fortress against age built,
I'd wink: pride overhaul and grits chanting,
You'll know where the lines came from,
The meanings, the meanings you've always voiced:
Me at the nethermost and you for methane, petroleum…
But the truth will surely nettle your expectations.
And I wasn't going, dying…I was just burdened.
Meaningless synthesis of added organic mass will wait, As I am not yet
into process.

Paraclete

The paraclete said it:
To forage through the dried banana leaves
Wasn't the worst part nor was the weaverbird's
Shits drops on their heads a comparable dread,
It was the call to dig the ditches, the canals,
After the forests and the savannah clearance,
The ritualistic respect for the evaporated
Souls and the sediments left by the souls as they
Flew to their everlasting worlds,
The grief of the bereft, the wails of the orphans,
Pricked one's ears like a sharp pointed pin
Driven into the softest of skins,
Yet a day went by to witness not a difference.
Afraid of invasion of nature, the dingy invite
Of sour cosmos, and the mixed approximations,
No one could guess the real cause of their plight.
They had to just wait as I see them vanishing,
Even me, the paraclete, helplessly stared...
As yester-years blew away the remaining souls.

None

I have been staring, really caring,
Thinking, murmuring and daring
To erase and polish my mellow airing.

The petards, the canon, the slicker
Avalanche and monsoon master,
Wispy and grizzled, still have me to pester.

Melodious as caterpillar but still a cantankerous
Arsonist, silly and scary the dragon fly, serious
And resolute the mantis, you guess the obvious!

I strive to have, please to drive, the queen
But bees being bearers how come they squirm?
Does the stink please, or can altruism be a scheme?

Before Pay Cheques

Sprawled on the couch three hours before
The real scene of the night, like a hipster
Basking in silly lustre, it was the night's
Invention and concealment to recount.

You'd think I was doing math if you'd seen
That dazzle of a calculator my hand,
Thinking I was at algebra to marks, but
I was one cheque away from the paupers
Circles: the sleepless nights at the plant,
The fading optimism and Rhodesian relegation.

I had counted days to cross the river
Safe and sound, dreams plunged and shredded
Into myriads of tatters, the grip of scholarly
Weaponry weakened, the sharpness of the brain
Slowed, the trickle and twinkle of my last
Words still had John say:
 "You'll make it thro' riches gate!"

PART IV

NATURE OF THINGS

Nature of Things

The petrel over the street post
Is the nature we want.
I may need it, but despised
Like a leper they say...
They say it's just a crow, a *black* bird,
The fear and love,
Scorn and praise always,
Come from me,
The day I wanted a drink, to be
Drunk like grandpa, who
Is downed by a mere wine's taste,
I drank marinade for a beer,
And a day later, adorned with marabou's
Feather, smothered, I breathed a pukka prolix,
'He's some', there was a scornful voice.

Accept This Truth

If proofs were the *Truth*, the maidens, the charwomen
Ogling with pompous milky owl's eyes would not
Whine, they'd breathe their chaos and abridge
Themselves.

I'd admit the proofs and all through exist behind,
Doubt me in your shrewd passage to churn
The toil abreast kingliness and forget it all.

If that shirt from that dirt, true embroidery, was the
The kingly hue, you'd not even bend to see me,
Do I wear any value?
I'm attired in all cribbed long johns.

If you speak and speed to see *all* first, and that
Quickness is the required reign, I'd not doubt
If I hail after you, or should I?
Your truth survives.

If you're adorned to shine by word and sight,
And prophesize more that Moses actually did,
'Blessing' me to the rear, wouldn't I understand why
I do fit eternally in the rear?
Well, yes, it's your festive invite for the day
You'd called me to festivity as camaraderie.

Nonentity

I will always be there, in my cryptic being,
Frisking every time, everywhere, but still

Finding nothing to see myself in like I did
Thousands of years ago, when I'd sip or gulp,

Scoop or lick the taste of nature's accolade, then presented
To the cinnamon one, the brave one, I was an egg then,

Now as I continue the search, here and there, now
And then, by me and others, I would want to …

Just break the silence with my spear, tearing
Souls open with my sparkling silver spear; it'll be that.

They'll then come for me like madmen and blow me
To grainy pieces, but like the chief's spear, shiny in bright
And searing tropical midday,

I know my search will shine, and it'll be even
When I'm seen and not there, found but lost:

A spear that doesn't kill yet painful and dazing.

Always Be Pain

All know the sun peeps
Earnestly and early from the east,
With that orange grace
It eases all into peace,
But who says that that bountifulness
Is from the evening, from the west?
 – no one thinks that some people have
That as central free will,
Still sealed, a fill of ill feelings,
Long done at the days, scholastic days,
Days of no accountability,
When the buffalo would be left scares,
Only the buffalo's meat was needed,
But all still say he looks magnificent,
Fine from dawn to dusk.

As then existing conscience
Manned the relegated animals,
Thomases were ubiquitous,
Not small and sure, all know that:
Elephant-hearted and rat-bodied,
All see that—pride—this
Giant partnered by a proud-less figure,
Did Descartes say they had no soul?
What about bishop's prayers?

The sacred secret of godliness milks the milkless
The righteous endures to see through the unbearable
With a miniature heart that oozes pukka friendliness.

All didn't go with pain to the wild, so is it my turn?
Or maybe we'll one day painfully sing alike.
Perhaps nature knows when, because the

Cinnamon ones have elastic hearts,
And we'll stay near her as friends, no less,
Because the aggressive buffalo is tamed!

The Hind-Island

I had called the priest the day I got sick,
Dad had told me a visit to the infirmary
Would ease the cramps and the hurricanes
In my head, but the visit couldn't guard me from
The anopheles' bites,
The nets were but jokes,
The plant leaves I was told to burn got the
Insects laugh at that folly,
I wished it wasn't a jest,
But I hate to blame if nothing deserves praises,
My old fathers remained here,
If only they had migrated and elaborated,
Some friends have said to me that
Dad cautioned me, 'look at testimonies dad,'
I had said,
The insects would be marching to
Their suicidal ends, now at least they can
Sip their meals in their peace,
Because I will always be here, the 'food,'
One day I will evolve, but what plight need I see?
The tropics and savannah would not save
The lion with hair shaped smooth,
The sheet above scotched by my hands,
I would have many skin ulcers,
But look! I know how to climb trees,
Does evolution mean I could fly?
Smile, I'll remain here on the last Island,
As I Die Slowly: fast live span.

Confession

Why can't I walk backwards
Not to see what lies ahead of me?
That sounds like a loser's resort,
But all I see makes me wonder,
Presented or sought, all speak the same,
If I vex street users or amuse them,
It all comes down to the same:
No one really cares!
But everyone wants to laugh, heartily,
I'll always say peace be upon them,
Walking backwards will show me
Who I was then, no one knowing,
I, a coward or a brave,
I'll pass all with the same timidity,
But not on these kingly streets,
But maybe yes if I soar like a madman
And win me some Samaritans,
I'll see how it all works out in the main,
My gods will not be happy though,
As I take some confusion as my heart,
I'll be warned, perhaps, by spear holding…
Oh, not angels, but…but by warriors,
Warriors dressed like pharaonic guards,
When Egypt was people and not the land,
My god will not be pleased, but thanks be to him/her,
He/she has no hell, because the seat is hotter than hell,
Loaded with molten aluminium fury, but there is he!
I will pay cows to kill and cleanse my soul
Because he invents no hell.

The Attorney's Words

I don't know
How long he will be?
From heat to cold,
From hell to haven,
And then back to hell again.
He defiled the open hospitality
And bit the finger that fed him!
Sure, the lines of nearness are close
By enumeration to his neighbours,
The equatorial forest's lives have open arms,
Thinking, yet not enough for a clear leap,
I didn't say we could be one,
Insistence crammed the summoned cord,
Though I compromised my will and
Tongue, they bounced for themselves,
Defiled but back they answered,
Now inside the box of bars.
For the equatorial brotherly clime
I'll have you wait...
God knows the length of your being,
The would-be your time of existence,
I had said a bent rightness and we
Got together with specicist thoughts,
Beings not on the same paces only space,
I'm sorry I only admit the contrivance,
The same old hand for your open vapity,
Thinking it's gone, but only the worldwide service.
Stay me!

For Your Face's Sake

Smile for the camera and smile
For your face, a little light while
We paint your bright face,
So that you can look, marvel at the pace
With which your face brightens:
The jingling ankle,
And the wink tightens.

Hat dropping like African hamlet huts' eaves,
Hair unkempt and wild as cat in the squeeze,
We need to make you look decent, respectable,
Civil, but the hat will crumple the neatness,
Your dusty, dark countenance smile will suffice not,
Remove the hat, 'because the flash and smile are not
Enough.'

At noon and still we'd failed, fading optimism,
But we'll not abandon aiding lighting the face,
That sparkling crystalline darkness, refined and divine,

Now, you should have seen the photo product
To dash your fading opposite desires.
Your brightness. Your dark, shiny face.

Natural Silence

In a desolate and dim, sullen cave,
Where arcadia life never have
A stripped existence,
There exists no crystal pence.

But in the dark sullen cave,
Pestilence mans, admitting no nerve.
Outside eyes pour ambivalence
Over the cave.
But only few eyes really glance.

The artic brother knows not its favor,
Although feigning, the chaperon never
Will her heart be known:
Cooks well,
Serves well,
Admonishes well,
Advises well.

The cave stoops in
Age,
Immaturity
And needs,
Her nights whistle purity,
But she's to be disinfected of contents,
The power of artic hearts fights pretense.

Always the Suffragan

The exiguous ivy would rally the
Thick of throng of citizens to whine,
The midst and the end of citizens will
Fan the ache over the new citizens,
Who'll squeeze the bottle?
It's the onerous feats ignored,
Though the republic sighs, belches, grins,
At times laughs...the truth is,
Everything in the reliquary would have the
Buffalo, the new citizens, relish nonentity,
For they eat from the same old hand,
Like the waters of the Nile upward marching,
It steps on buffaloes for mercies, cruel and crude,
Citizens' rudeness is the crystal divide,
Tomorrow everyone breathes but dubious,
Teeth will be shown for pretentious everything,
The laughs for pretentious everything,
Asking what new and old citizens did mean,
And who are they? It's an irony!
They needed to laugh the cries,
And then cry the laughs,
When all show their colours as shiny teeth,
Not the folly of their covering,
The suffragan, new citizens now manning,
Old citizens will have you ask:
"What just happened?"
"Not always the suffragan!"
Said the new citizens.

Superior Pen

Disparity brightly striking,
Nature's exposition wickedly clear,
Phenomenally polar still,
But he still wanted
To expose the sunk
And sung difference, glaringly,
Maybe to distant himself
From the old island,
The island, powerful and iniquitous
Like an annoyed icky leopard,
But no one thought
He was part of the old island!
The count was lost in history,
But the glare and flare are implicit.

They saw him with bountiful
Magnificence of Shakespearean
Astuteness,
He gripped the pen, erased, effaced
The errors but put them back in,
No one dared a critical speech, criticism,
He painted their opposite small
Though happy with an old, rickety ancient
Nightmares the island has always basked in.
But why draw the obvious difference
And think himself clean, the best upper hand?
Because that hand is not ethically defended,
But maintained dreadfully, unconscionably,
The giant, the island, fell and descended slowly
Why sill fear the weak?

The Mountain

A witty mountain,
A golden treasure,
Imaginary treasure, a soothing treasure,
A lost, star, a non-existent miracle,
There it exists not, the gleeful gold mountain, but
Who has the universe in his motherly palms?
And who, fearless and with piercing eyes,
And who crave *treasureable* testimony?
The tested son? The groomed son?
The defiant, the learned, and the timid,
Drum their chests bloodless and say it all
That there is *not* a gold mountain!

They ride high,
They sky high,
And they brag and sigh,
Strength in all colours and shapes,
Strength in all measures of depths,
But then their desires wane,
And their hope's flames die,
Fluffed by the search...
But Alas! the gold mountain smiles,
The flamboyance of the invincible villain,
Not reachable not understandable,
Perhaps somewhere, ululating:
 "Ooh! Ooh! Can't fine me!"

The fool will not be known,
The smartest will stand abreast fools,
The magnificent parity heavy and yielding,
The smart wooed to whine; the fools fly the festive
Mood, and the end never comes,

The end comes,
And we all know,
There is *not* a gold mountain
But there *is* a gold mountain.

Styrofoam Gadgets

Their loads stuffed with Styrofoam
Gadgets, and convinced, coerced to believe
They were carrying heavy metals,
Though lacking the chiefly chintz
And prime Chippendale, they found
Their way through like rainwater through
The gutter into the drainage,
There was a blow out of foxy wits, condensed
And absorbed by preserved cotton-like chinchilla
Now that the chloroform conspiracy
Watched and washed, and wrong belief straightened,
Herbal feeling abandoned,
On some, stars the belief, but still they will eke for living
Even if discretion rules by imposition.
Again, like threads of lightening in a pitch
Black and stormy night, they
Will shimmer, when it becomes
A Styrofoam and not a metal!

Jesus Loves You!

He, in that remarkable sermon looks white,
But he writes to behave like he is wise
To the poor who look nothing dark but light,
But all now run after prophecy day and night,
To beg for honour, forgiveness and fame: is that right?
This leaves me with the question to the devil:
Why are we the same?

They curve the frame to have me resemble
The best in the phrase, gathered to humble
Me and the word that makes my head noble,
They decide and give me, like police, I assemble
All those 'honorary' badges received with the terrible
Acceptance of a man with no choice but to crumble,
And sleep tortured by quilt (enforced) to wake up simple,
But still, at the end I'm left with the question: Devil,
Why are we the same?
Jesus. Answer me!

Unconsciously Subjugated

When she called the doctor she wasn't accepted
the same. Something familiar of her was expected.

She went to the store and thought she had a dollar,
but fifty cents she was told it was, her defined collar.

At the cinema she wanted to have fun, enjoyment
as blessing, 'the movie's complex,' echoed disappointment,

She went to the church; to God she would humbly yell
and pray, but being as hard to handle as a baby eel,

A voice had said, 'don't be angry, God is merciful,'
but she scuttled off as she couldn't be that careful,

Cosmic weight fixed as a bestowal, tripled the heaviness
as her paces dwindled before the church pane stillness.

The Transistor

When I came closer to the transistor,
It was oiled to complications and still
Hoarded...
I tried the primitive ballistic
Incantations to have the way drilled
Through the cover of the storage building,
But the constraining metals budding
Through the entrance of the already hidden
Transistor store, wailed for my daylight stop.
I had to; I had to break from this labyrinthine
Match to uphold consciousness of the
that fortress,
That meridian always
On the other smiley side, the side
Were natures' needs are met with
The ease of free fall.
When I wanted to use the transistor,
I was swarmed with smiles and there
The transistor had me heard.
When it malfunctioned, I had to turn it
Where it gets oiled and I stand in the
Same swamp, soused to the neck,
And the labyrinthine way grins until
The transistor comes.

Recondite

Look at me, mysterious as
Recondite and inchoate discoverer,
To whistle the sound to have you attentive,
To have you apprehensive
But cheerfully guarded,
You have seen Tokyo vibrant
And inventive, humble but procuring
Chill of unwanted acceptance,
Now, do we have to see her, accept her?
You already have the niche, enviable
And immovable as Everest,
But Tokyo's testimony has us think:
I remained covered by moss, dust storm
and match into the bleakest meaninglessness.
You have seen the mystery I swim in:
Incomprehensible like Beijing Meridian,
Your silver face and supple organism
I will want to like.

Empty Ode

Incomplete,
Inconclusive,
No reign is peeping;
And the safe enclave evasiveness
Jarred,
So now we can all sing alike:
'Lord!' we will pray.

PART V

ON INNOCENCE AND WONDER

Let's Talk About It

It's just the talk, don't squirm
And don't dread it, for the style
And seal will drive along the lines you drew,
And consciousness had us see the unseen,
For the talk demands energy more than
The design of its invention.

We will wait for the minstrel to enliven
Our climate if the talk paralyzes us,
The poems have to be selflessly stylistic,
Tonally moodless, thematically pointless,
For if not, we would all squirm
In discomfort as the talk unsettles us.

The songs have to bind us together and paint
Our faces as fertile laugher plants,
And bring our hands together,
The theme should always be pointless,
Settling and naïve,
For naivety is the master of togetherness.

Discretion not translatable to morbid denial,
Not exposed as concealed hypocrisy either,
Will be discarded because discretion translates,
And we should be as open as air above oceans,
And avoid the enigmatic philosophy of Christ,
Because, it is time for us to talk about it:
The talk.

Definition of the Minds

There was a day, a day I thought of minds
And I sniffed a rough definition, a definition
That saw me assume my cribbed pilaster as rara avis.
They had occupied the hall to the brim,
But there I thought I could blend in,
 But, yes, the minds had to be defined.

The long winding and meandering past path,
Closed at the end of the search, with all the
rendition, and salvaged chlorophyll freshness,
Was the innocence I wanted to exhort,
But all crumbled when the minds were defined:
But to be singly lauded was classic mockery.

I came close to the experiment when I did it
myself, like a drop of ink in a harmless paper,
I had shown the way. It has been centuries
Since then and the contentment is refined, redefined
And I sit under my orange tree on the Nile bank,
sniffing the scent and scenery as I wait for
The definition of whatever minds.

Everlasting Smiles

We could have walked and walked
Till the bleak, quiet, wide and abysmal African night give
Way to the African orange morning,
It was the same souls we'd revered that we feared, the red balls
Of the occident and the best had rained on us a week before.
The few who tightly clinked to their receding souls limped—
Limped for the glimmer of hope that the morning shine
Ahead bloomed with flamboyance of kickable dreams.

We could have fought and fought
Till the loud, thunderous, angry and sanguine foes' annihilator
Blows off the last oppressed souls after the horizon brightens,
Now those remaining few 'othered' souls are a nuisance,
Headaches that remained rekindled the then dying master' hiccups,
The sanguine could have had the land, stretching and stretching,
Straddling and embracing from all flanks of the Nile,
 It was and still the same bone that's always been the dreaded
cause,
We all need the land now,
The servants and the masters cry alike,
The thraldom of the sisterly south is the dilemma.

We could have laughed and laughed
Till the altruistic, the pious, the respectful, philanthropic cinnamon
Countenance, engrave on the statute the emblem of togetherness,
The sanguine could've had the pearls and the honey to himself,
I know caring for the bees is my job, but now we'll all be servile
Because being a master is a leap I cannot afford,
So you might as well climb down the stairs,
I am big you know and going up would be
A task, like a pipe that'd drain my coffers dry.

The Southern Bird

I have been a bird, a crow, an eagle,
A weaverbird, a dove, but one thing
Evaded me: the owner of my being,
Me, the bird of the south... wondering,
Perhaps he dodged the query of my consciousness,
I think my owner did just that as I am a bird.

I have been in a free egg, the egg cracked
And I silted out, happy and dazzling as
A cleanse gourd of a snazzy chief gaiety,
Flying in passion of the sky that knows no limits.
To the East, West, North and my beloved South:
Which was all an inhabitable dark's paradise,
Savannah plain, where, I, the bird, *trespassed*.

I have always sung wide and audible,
The South echoed my innocent melodious tenderness
Across the tropics, above the welcoming mysteries of
Rain forest, the domain of the kind primitive,
To the West I had the Nile smile in a gentle familiari-
ty,
Her file of charges awaits my seasonal flying over her
Charges, I believe, from the owner of my *being*,
Just because I am a bird.

I have always sipped from the mug of nature's token,
Knowing not that the bird had a father, a mother
Though not any husband or wife in naturalness,
I wanted to have one to love and cherish,
But the rain's invasion, the sun's scotching spears,
And the wild's race with me, had me see that I'm

parentless,
Yet the owner's mystery wasn't answered,
The birds' parents protect the bird, but I was left
To perch on a burnt, felled and a desolate tree,
Just because I'm not only a bird, but a *Southern Bird*.

The cashier

It was the morning of thanks giving,
I'd no where to go to, no specialty to
Eat, no specialty call, but I had visited
The store to balloon my deflating refrigerator:
Cereal, canned drinks, the red meat and peanut,
All characterized my arrival at the blue counter.
The lady of the country on the counter, pallid, jubilant
With oriental bracelets invading her left arm,
French accent and puzzling smile worn
And not understood; she asked me
If I wanted everything I'd brought,
Incapable I might have looked,
But friendlier should I always remain.
She smiled and I did nothing but the same.
I didn't even know I could afford them,
The trail of guilt had followed me,
Like a refined, defined gentlemen of metropolis,
I behaved like an English gentleman:
Truthful outside, lying inside!

PART VI

PRAISES AND DEDICATIONS

A Crown in A Man's Heart

Papa wasn't sure of it when
I called home in 99; he'd slaughtered a hen.
I sat under a mango tree and a cassette
Player on a rickety wooden table, the set
Of African voices of Congo, East African
Gospel beat, had me think I was home, but can
There be cogency in my reserved psyche? Like
A victorious imperialist I'd sat, every wish in light,
It was just comforting shades, Brother'd brought
Mangoes heaved on a big *sufuria,* he never bought
Them, he'd claimed the ubiquitous trees in the *River County,*
But when the quiet one homed again to his country
Three latter and a goat lost her life, dad wished
I stayed close to them, but fate wouldn't listen, I reached
The furthest abyss of personal recollection, oh sure!
He wasn't sure I'd be *here,* but I can't say if obscure
Or crystal, Dad first smelt the cosmic air in my absence,
And I wished he could cease inhaling in my presence,
It wasn't to be it; I hear dark-cinnamon voices every time
And nothing pushes me further then dad's verse, inclined
To have me the steps, the strict originality of his chord
And the natural appeal I describe not isn't my accord.
I hope to be back under my mango tree
Even if I can't see dad in a solace glee

My Brothers and My Neighbours

The years swiftly fled by
Like planes with supersonics,
But I still see mama wearing a dress
She had forty years ago,
My brother had promised her
A house,
A land,
A car,
Clean water, electricity...

Mama's still in the dark wearing rags,
Her soul wearing away in heat and age,
She walks to fetch water but my brother
Lives in abundance,
He quarrels with
My elder brother, wrangling for
Riches, and mama cries, ashamed
At her womb's making.

My mum had her friends laugh at her:
'You were better than us forty year ago!'
But she never blames her womb...why?
Like a lioness in the jungle, her will's grits steers
Her through hardship, neglect and mockery,
She was very wealthy then, but the...

The neighbours took her wealth,
But my brothers had promised her
More...
More...
And more...
Now mum stays the same,

98

I cry in sorrow, shame and despair,
Because mama is dying…
The neighbours who did it blamed my brothers,
but my brothers blame the neighbors,
I blame no one, but just living.

Dodo Speaking

Without You I'll Not Be Seen

Tell me the truth, tell me what you feel.
I'm not a ghost fixed in your body
As just that small magical man
Who knows your inner workings.
Tell me I don't assume, tell me you feel it,
And tell me I'm wrong...
Tell me I'm not.

I seem to hold a five hundred-year
Old knife of yesterdays anger and wounds,
But you oiled me into an indoctrinating darkness,
Maybe I'm the darkness and least
Can you see in the darkness.

The science of optics says the light the object
Reflects gives the object its phenomenology,
To appear, to be seen in its magical essence,
But unless you shine on me, on my darkness,
I'll never be seen; I'll never appear...
Deep in the bottom, at the end of the bedrock.

Even if I'm saved to the top without you,
I'll never be seen save you shine on me,
Though you conscionably polish me to reflect light,
You miss my finer details, my Fanonian distortion.
So how dare I hold a knife against you?
Because without you, I'll not be seen!

I Only Need a Quarter, Not a Loonie

On the other side of the street stood I, and laughs
A man on the other, his cup expectant though thanking
Passers-by more than the holder could,
"How do such things happen?" said a beauty out of a cab,
Her silky, golden hair fanning the environment
With overt *show off*, her violet satchel disappearing
In her expensive top hue,
"It's only laziness, look how strong he is?"
Said her man, wearing nothing but coloured by folly,
A folly, hidden by the pretty face, the wow cars, the hip fun...
Those were the markers of his disdaining existence.
"Have a good day," the man's cup said,
But the girl's man darkened the smile on the cup's face,
Closing his car's door, he briskly swayed into the hotel,
Rolled back seconds later with loonies and tossed
Them into the cup like a basketball star in the all-stars' *show
off*.
The cup stood tilted, loonies went flying onto the street,
The 'Samaritan' fumed, the cup fumed, but the cup's owner
Laughed, picked up his tilting cup, showing his amputee
Left leg, and heartily, quietly and inaudibly said:
"I only needed a quarter, not a loonie!"

By a Woman or a Man, I Am the Same

I'm not only adorned,
I'm the colour,
I not only like being adorned,
I'm nothing without it.

Money's the cellular unit of my brain,
I don't know what neurons mean,
But to my soul smothered the claim,
For without money,
I'd not be seen,
Am I bright?

I came from a woman and I like women,
I'm defined by parents: mum and dad,
All come to the same thing,
 But like a vagabond I'll always frisk to show
that I'm from a woman and a man.

It's preciousness that'd long evaded me,
Poor me should always be pardoned!
My oxymoronic existence was there; I'd seen it,
But Mississippi and Congo were too wide to cross.
That was centuries before.

Now, say now!
From all flanks of a woman called parity,
I managed to have a bicycle,
Colored to make me visible, conspicuous,
But they say I like things,
Big, Extravagant, And Vacuous!

Tropical Trumpets

Those decades never called supplication,
Now it's the path we'll never sanction,
They'll twist and feast in your palms,
Stone-piety mocks but pays the alms,
The then horns below the dessert
Fixed your call to assets
The day you circled the hill
The ants gathered. It wasn't a chill,
But they broadened your horizon
To caress the tropics, a baton,
With glorious bastion to rip
All that ants had built but ant's weak grip
And hurting stinks were only to burn
In the tropical heat as you had the pipe in hand.
Though they blew horns and faced nowhere,
You fixed their heads to *somewhere*,
At night, in dry seasons, they watched in unison,
The moon and the cross for inspiration,
 Religiously, which was the best?
The dawn or the dusk?

Crossing Our Rivers

If I have been crawling and you wanted
Me dashing, I will tell you the corrobaree
I staged for you was a sign, perhaps
The pleasantry for you the sun, the Jupiter of
Beings, but my school had begun when
I couldn't cross Mississippi.
The Congo lords were crude, pallid and angry,
I wasn't to get vexed, it wasn't my line, they'd said,
The Nile's elegance was mine but never mine,
The cross and the moon wrangled for me and mine,
Till this day, they still do, but like all our slums' guttersnipes,
The epitome of all sordid plights and flights,
The missed fortune enjoyed my slow speed,
The lightening struck and I'd no shelter,
I'd always mentally thickened and weakened
The will till I was confused;
The heart Fanonian I'd become, fresh and smiling,
With no deterrence and charms of change,
Followed a designed doctrinaire,
The range of acolytes manned that procurement,
The past punch was strong but was it worth *the* smile?
No one recollects it or want to, now,
We can all sniff and blow new breeze.
It whistles by as we pretentiously peep!

Brother's Heart Booth

Iron heart, the stamp of
Purity grits, surmounts the
Reflective endurance like the humble Nile,
It swallows all the waters, rejecting any abhorrence
Of the claimants that carries no thickness,
But It still holds on to disdainful ventures,
Not procured for real humanitarian cause
But to defame the native brothers, 'cause
The truth is not known but told, the venturers think,
But we all had and heard the crying tears,
Not only did we cry tears,
But how do we weigh the hearts and
Pain of tears that cried the more we cried?
 Ask me not, you may say!
But I tell you brothers, thy will
Prevails when the elephant assumes
The heart of a rat, but not to squeeze
Himself into the hole dead, but to only push
The realistic button, to say, "Ha! Ha!
Brother I hear you, and want no anathema,
But plant me a room in your heart,
I know you can, your heart looks
Minutes, an itsy bitsy,
But I say NO!
You sound mean but I know,
Deep in you the little black cat is calling:
'Forgiveness in the brother's heart!'"

We Can Do It Emily

We don't eat the same, but the
Revivifying food we can eat
Together, on your four-generation
Purple dinning table, which's as old as your
Grandma, who died a month ago.

There exist no irrevocables, says she, remember?
But there exists undeniable dogma,
Of which I lay prostate and helpless,
It's thousand times my weight;
What do you think?

But hope there is, she'd said, you know,
'How and what is it?' Emily, you'd asked,
'Call your friends'! she'd said,
'And push the demon,'

But muss still rules, are we unable?
Our collective weight is a quarter
Of the demon, I know,
So we need strength, Emily, please,
I need us to eat together...to eat
That mussel and toss off the mustard.

Thök de Ka

Kuir ë Garang is a South Sudanese poet, writer and author cur-rently living in Calgary, Alberta. For more information about the author and all his writings, visit his website at

www.kuirthiy.com